ON HER FACE THE LIGHT OF LA LUNA

PROVINCETOWN POETS, VOLUME V

Series Editor: Christopher Busa

ON HER FACE THE LIGHT OF LA LUNA

by Mairym Cruz-Bernal

PROVINCETOWN ARTS PRESS

ACKNOWLEDGMENT is made to the periodicals where the following poems first appeared:

Boston Review:	"Cutting Pablo's Hair"
	"The Pain of Pleasure"
	"Playmates in the Bathtub"
Provincetown Arts:	"Excesses"

Most of these poems were written during residencies in the MFA program at Vermont College of Norwich University. I thank the director, Roger Weingarten, and my teachers, Christopher Noël, Susan Mitchell, Jack Myers, and particularly Deborah Digges, who first named me poet and gave me permission to set the word free. I am also grateful to Carolyn Forché and her husband Harry for entering my house in Puerto Rico and remaining in my memory. To my friend Gretchen Ramirez, a sensitive spirit encouraging me to go all the way, through, thank you.

This book is funded in part by the Massachusetts Cultural Council, a state agency that receives support from the National Endowment for the Arts. Additional support has been provided by contributions from foundations, corporations, and individuals.

Published by PROVINCETOWN ARTS PRESS, INC.
650 Commercial Street, Provincetown, MA 02657

FIRST EDITION

Designed by Ewa Nogiec
Frontispiece by Michelle Weinberg

PAPER ISBN: 0-944854-22-2
CLOTH ISBN: 0-944854-23-0

Library of Congress Catalog Card Number: 96-71163

PRINTED IN USA

For my daughter, Mariana Emilia
and the savage woman growing inside her

CONTENTS

Did you not know?—
   The moment you became the moon,
   You became the most visible light in the sky.

—Jalaluddin Rumi

ON HER FACE THE LIGHT OF LA LUNA

FIRST LETTER

Let me invent a world in these letters.
This world that I have does not serve me.
The sea, too immense,
in desolation.
A sea that goes and comes,
growing fingers to reach you.
Let me steal the sense from you, make you crazy,
madden you, seduce you, and like this, like this,
even if I never have you again.

How many things I could tell you tonight.

Tell you for example
  that every time I cry
    I feel that my chest wants to come out
      as if it were a dove
        twisting inside me.

Tell you for example
  that when I think about you
    I want to steal your breath.
The wind awakens my nipples:
  such are your fingers or your mouth
    that, humid, kisses my body.

Tell you that I am sad,
  that I was born like this and like this I feel.

Tell you nothing,
  in the end, I have nothing.
A life lived. I have nothing.
A pen in my hand,
an ink that writes my thoughts.

(translated from the Spanish by the author)

CARTA PRIMERA

Déjame inventarme un mundo en estas cartas.
Es que este mundo que tengo ya no me sirve.
Es demasiado el mar que rodea a esta isla,
un mar inmenso,
desolador.
Un mar que va y que viene
y que yo imagino puedan crecerle dedos
para llegar hasta ti.
Déjame robarte el sentido, volverte loco,
enloquecerte, seducirte, y así, así,
aunque nunca llegue a tenerte.

Cuántas cosas podría decirte esta noche.

Decirte por ejemplo
  como bailan las nubes por encima de mis pechos.
Tratar de explicarte
  que el mar es un amante
  que me toca completa sin besarme.

Decirte por ejemplo
  que cuando pienso en ti
  quisiera robarte el aliento.
Como el viento levanta mis pezones,
  me parece que son tus dedos
  o tu boca que húmeda
  me besa el cuerpo.

Decirte que estoy triste,
  que nací así y que así siento.

Decirte nada,
  en fin, nada tengo.
Una vida vivida, nada tengo.
Una pluma en la mano,
una tinta que escribe mis pensamientos.

THE SILVER WOMAN

I remind myself I am in the city where civilization started,
that I am a woman and that I have a name. I remember
my name. Remembering does not stop my dance.
I raise my head and round my lips
opening all the mouths of the silver woman's body
till she is no longer in front of me, till I swallow her
into my own body. The mirror is broken.
I know now I carry a woman inside me,
someone who was thrown into a mirror.
I don't know if I should act as if I were crazy.

Swing, maybe. I grasp my knees, move my body
back and forth. I feel the dizziness of a wild dance.
I press my head to my knees and smell even the intimate
odors of my body. The woman is beautiful.
How can a beautiful woman·suffer so much imprisoned
in that mirror? She looks at me while I dance,
touches the corners of the mirror to touch me.

I had to be scared, but I don't remember.
I surrendered all my senses of logic to be calm
in front of her. I want to give her space to exist.
In the obscurity of the hall, in the midst
of a strange cloud of dust, I sit like a student
on the rug looking up to the tall woman
in front of me. But she inclines her body
to resemble my height. I am motionless,
legs crossed, hands poised on my knees, each side
with each side and I look at her eyes and think
what would I do if I were crazy.

I walk slowly. Nothing to do yet I find no rest.
My own voice coming from the outside says *Mira*.
In front of me, mirrors. As my body quiets,
a woman is forming her body out of smoke: her contours,
her wide hips, her long arms stretching
as if she had been bent for ages. A silver woman
moving her petrified soundless lips.

I started to walk down the narrow hall
of this cheap hotel when I felt my head bending,
my eyes facing the navy-blue rug. I started counting
the dots of dirt like fat in an open skin.
I think, how would I act if I were crazy.

CUTTING PABLO'S HAIR

What must I do? I see nothing but obscurities
on every side. Shall I believe I am nothing?
Shall I believe I am God?

— PASCAL

Pablo's long hair seems like pieces of rope.
He has not bathed for months, and for a year
he has been heaping trash. Says that God talks to him,
that he is the chosen son that will save the world.
But Pablo doesn't want to be the chosen son
when he can be God. He knows that ministers don't want only
to preach. They want to own their people's soul.
That's why they speak differently.
Pablo speaks with a sophisticated accent.

I wonder what language God speaks. Pablo says:
"When the Spirit enters a body, that body
becomes someone and speaks in different tongues
that no one can understand, like God." I can't understand
people either. Pablo has been quiet.
People ignore quiet people.
Pablo has spent half his life asleep. When he was awake
the people he loved died. He was six years old
when his younger and only sister died. A cocktail of sadness
and anger navigates within him. He cries.
He has been left without his other person. Since that time
his father started drinking and hitting his mother.
Pablo wanted to kill his father.

When Pablo turned ten his father was killed by a car.
Pablo's father was twenty-six, his own age now.
He was sad but he did not cry. A father turns into
an alcoholic by the immense sadness of losing
his only daughter. A son who thinks that the one
who father loved was sister. "What about me?
What am I here for?" I imagine Pablo's thoughts.
But he remembers he wanted to kill his father.

Pablo is a person who is not a person.
He needs to invent a person to be someone, God.
He wants to be isolated from people,
to meditate like Jesus in the desert and like
Jesus in the desert he is tempted. A voice
orders him to throw himself from a precipice.
Another voice tells him that he is elected by God
to save the world. But Pablo believes he is God.
He keeps his shit in his pants.

Suppose, that just for a day someone could get
Christ's feces and keep it. Everything that comes out
of Pablo's body is holy. He won't clean his sweat.
He won't flush his sperm. Like Christ,
he will stay without a woman. He won't shave.
He won't cut his nails. Pablo will not comb his hair,
nor speak right. But when I ask him
if he knows what elements are important
for vegetation to live, he says: "Solar light, water

and oxygen." When I ask him why it gets cooler at nights,
he says: "Because the sun is turned off."

I wanted to do the impossible for Pablo,
but the impossible can not be done.
I wanted to tell Pablo's life in the past tense,
to make these happenings history.
"Can you cut these voices demanding me to have a someone
inside?" Pablo asks me, "I want my thoughts
to belong to me. Can you cut my hair?"
I can cut your hair, Pablo. Let me cut your hair now.

HEADACHES

Maybe I'm sick. I don't want to talk
about my head or a tumor in it.
In the dream the high school girls
were wearing diapers.
I was one of them but I didn't have diapers on,
something to hold what comes out of my body
like papers holding words.
We are going to die. Our bodies,
worms.
Nothing else.
I've been always waiting for the next life
to become the someone I wish to be.
Waiting
and letting my life be
in service, the servant,
the caretaker, the mother,
the giver.
Now I must die and I don't believe
in an afterlife.

Alone, having coffee,
I don't want to be seen
to have to wear that instant mask of smiles
that says everything is okay.
I am tired of my makeup
and blow-drying my hair.
It's too much time with my face in the mirror,
tired of these headaches
and the things I don't do.
I am tired of this enormous pride
saying I don't need my father

when I see him in every tall and handsome man
that walks around. I am tired of this headache of pretenses
   Not tonight, my head, you know it hurts or
      Let's eat out tonight . . .
   No dear, I know you are tired.

I am so considerate
with everybody else.
My daughter is one year old.
She's crying. Her eyes pressed and closed,
her mouth wide open with a scream inside.
She's just playing.
I wonder how often I do that
that she learned so quickly
the game of dishonesty.
But this headache is real.
Nobody can see it but it is in my brain,
as real as the veins
palpitating
on the sides of my head.
Real as the tumor interrupting
the passage of my life. I'll be thirty next autumn.
It's okay to finish now.
Age means nothing.
I'm leaving.
Maybe I'll have a parking ticket
pressed to the wipers of my new car.
A ticket I don't expect to pay.

This is just a game to pretend to die.

BORROWED PASSION

I whisper,
my body pressing yours: "Give me something."
Coming back from wherever you are,
you open your eyes, turn,
embrace
not me, not the voice who asked you for something,
but the only thing you can have in your hands.

You touch me.
Thinking you are exciting me
you excite yourself.
Borrowing passion, instead of giving.
You put your mouth on my mouth
to feel some lips, any tongue.
You come inside my body
knowing my ova will not be fertilized.
You want to give me a sperm
I can not use anymore,
like the aftershave balm your daughter gave you
for you birthday you won't use to shave
your long white and gray beard.
You rest, tired,
pull your body
out of my body.
You lie on the bed
with your back against me
asking me to embrace you.

I move,
embrace you.
I wait some minutes.
I know what I want.

I whisper: "Give me something."
You open your eyes. Tenderly,
you give me now the front of your body,
your face, your chest,
your abdomen, the front part of your legs.
You give me your eyes looking at me, more,
staring at me, questioning me.
Easily, like baby-children falling asleep,
I open and close, open and close,
open and finally I close my eyes.

THE HANDKERCHIEF

The white handkerchief on your desk
reminded me of a time when I could not
accept anything from anyone. I was repelled by the touch
of another human being. I was eating a framboise ice cone.
Its thickness was retained in my mind like blood
inside my body. The cone started to melt and it dripped
covering my right hand. It was Sunday morning
in front of the Presbyterian Church,
and I was thirteen years old.

The service ended at midday. I felt the sun
beading my brow. He was bored,
attractively bored. His eyes fixed
on my dripping cone, smiling to himself.
For a fraction of a second
I didn't know what to do and he handed me
his white handkerchief.

I could not tolerate that color
dirtying his handkerchief and then inside his pocket.
He insisted.
I felt a sudden delinquent purpose at play and rejected him
without batting an eyelash.
But the pressure of his thought made
the actual holding of the cone unfeasible and I
threw it on the grass and ran to the sink
to wash my hands. When I came back I saw his eyes
still there, gradually de-abstracting.

His eyes appeared to jettison everything.
When he moved again,
it was as though from marionette strings.
I did not collapse into that world
neither did I grow up ever accepting a handkerchief.

He flinched back to his place.
I never saw him again.

For some years I walked
adorning my own coquettish solitude, learning
to lace all my acts with a feminine mockery. Becoming
a flower, a lilting almost sonorous bouquet, indulging
in the intoxication of a perfect fragrance. Trailing
at my pace, a mingled scent of flowers and flesh.

SHADOWS

In honor of a white hair growing
in the middle of my head, I will not
bleach my hair anymore. I want to see it.
I have forgotten my natural color.
I wonder why so many changes in me, so many coming backs.
My grandmother came for a week. When she left,
it was as if she were saying good-bye.
I feel she's dead.
Yesterday I went to see my mother.
Her legs failing her, her steps slow.
Her father died when she was inside my grandmother's womb.
She always remembers this.

One day, a long time ago, she was fighting with my father
in front of four witnesses, something happened,
she started talking like a little girl,
I have a father, I have a father.
He protects me, he makes two long braids in my hair.
Cuddling her hands, sweating. I thought we lost her,
but she came back from her childhood.
She imagined the tenderness of a father, never leaving her,
always protecting her. My older brother
started caressing her forehead, wanting to clear up her mind,
to bring her back to being our mother. I went to my father,
who had moved to another room. I asked him, speechless,
he said not to worry. I knew he was worried himself.
For so many days he was gone, away, somewhere.

. . . but I married a man

I press my eyes to see stars of many colors.
Time is ending and there is something I must do.
Fear breathes through my pores. I am never afraid.
Today I am afraid of dying. I don't want to see a doctor.
I press my eyes to see stars of many colors
and imagine those colors and imagine those stars.
My house is a mountain with cool breeze.
My house is a tree with wide arms for my rest.
Green arms, green stars,
a green mountain blossoming in winter.
But I am so apart from my house, from the music
of that piano I used to play as a child.
A piano that was bought for me and *Für Elise*.
Now my fingers are gnarled and bent.
I should have kept that piano, those pieces of music.
I wanted to be a mother like my mother.
I wanted to have a father forever . . .

THE SEARCH

The stars are eyes.
Someone else exists, softer,
more tender than people here on the earth.
I don't know what those eyes
will see in me. I don't know
if they see me the way I see
myself, as someone will see a semblance
in the mirror,
like my baby-daughter,
who while crawling looks at me through the mirror
and thinks it's me and laughs and starts
crawling again towards the mirror.
Then she hears my voice calling *Mariana*.
She looks the other way and sees me
                                                      again.
She looks to the mirror and looks back into me.
She feels the real me, and crawls
towards it. Who am I anyway?
For my daughter, for the stars looking at me tonight,
for my son who closes his eyes and takes me into his dreams,
his last vision of someone on earth before he departs?
Who am I? For the man who waits
till I serve him dinner,
and clean the table, close the windows,
the doors, who waits for my body to get into his bed,
for whom I am also his last imagination

of a human before his rest?
Who am I for myself? The one I see in the mirror
while brushing my teeth or the one the stars see,
or the mother, or the maid, or the cook,
or the wife acting in bed?
I see no pattern to find me, to distinguish me.
But I am anyway
and I will be even more soon.

THE PAIN OF PLEASURE

I didn't take notes to remember.
I forget to take notes. I forget
my tape recorder. I don't keep my memories.
Everything is lost, every memory hidden
in the depth of my dreams. But my dreams
are always too far, I forget them.
It was only last night that my daughter
woke up with a strange kind of cough
and when I went back to my bed,
closed my eyes, I saw I was trying
to close a door
but the bolt was stuck.
I called someone, a man, to help me
fix the bolt. Our hands touched
by chance, not by wish.
It felt dirty, like something sticky
was left on my hands after each rub,
something sticky in my hands I don't
want there. A door I can not close
to keep my son from knowing what happens
in my bed, to know my ambivalence,
my yes I want and my yes I don't want.
I don't want him to know I give my love
to another man. The other night he heard
my noises. He thought it was pain
and not pleasure. I thought he was sleeping
and not listening. And maybe I feel guilty
because I can't share this pleasure
with him, the person I love most.

CHRONICLE OF AN ABANDONMENT

Ay! The slaps on my mouth that prohibited me
from telling Papa how sad I had been all day without him.
How it hurts, that last one given to me
when he was leaving forever. There I stayed
dumb so much that I had to invent the verse
to say that my chest was hurting.

I spoke
never again.

Last night my father called with charges to my house
to say they were praying for me
in his church because of the problems I had.
What problems? I ask. If I don't die of hunger,
if my children are not dying of cancer,
if they were abandoned by their father, so what?
I was too.

And look at me, I can drink coffee,
I have an umbrella to shield me from the water,
a brassiere to sustain my breasts and cloth to cover my skin.
What problems? I said to this man from whom I inherited
the last name that I dropped as soon as I could.
Now I carry my children,

a prince and a princess,
and I cover them with the mantle of my blood.
My blood that bathes them with strength.
It is too soon for them to be ignored,

and I decided, *Basta*!
I am left with a mute smile, with some tears
already dried, but with a roaring spirit.
How much loneliness on a wide mattress,
on linen sheets stained with weeks of not loving.
I stayed alone with myself to play my body with my fingers,
to do with me whatever I wanted
even to tattoo a mark on my skin.

I have aged.
I forget about myself and who I am.
I forget about my children, about old lovers in dreams.
I color my nails and let them grow.
I don't have to defend myself from myself,
from my desires to scratch men's backs
from the hatred of being penetrated,
of being hurt
till all the blood empties from my body.
I am letting my hair grow
so when I put my head down it covers my face
and nobody will see the dark rings under my eyes
or the shame of my red lips.

(translated from the Spanish by the author)

ON MY KNEES

A short bronze man walks on his knees through *el Zócalo*,
  to the atrium of *La Catedral de la Virgen de Guadalupe*,
    holding a baby-girl in his hands, paying a promise
      to *la virgencita* because his daughter was healed.

I am ruined.
People sitting down, standing up,
                            walking.
Faces savoring hunger.
I see bodies that will never uncurl from postures of hurt.

How long does the break in human flesh stay open?
  When does it start to heal?
    Will it ever be dissolved?

I am contaminated with their stitches.

Inside *La Catedral* I light a candle.
Outside, it is not yet sunrise.
I walk on my knees on the sand
                            where my passage leaves no trace.

And I am this moment the abortion of a new day,
  this vomit of the ocean.

IRIS

I don't know Iris but she has a beautiful name.
When she was little she used to stand on the tip
of her toes to be lifted.
As a woman she stands open to be used.

At school she meets her history teacher,
sits near his desk and feels the awakening
of her twelve-year-old body.
His hands move along her thighs
and touch her vagina discretely.
She never tells anyone.

It is this same man who in three years
places his thorn-finger into her
while his other covers her mouth.
She cries and bleeds.
Although hurt, she feels she belongs,
naming her future.

I am my name . . . what if this is the only thing I am
and it's broken? An adopted child, at twenty-two
my mother committed suicide. What am I supposed to do
now that I am twenty-two?

This time, just before she decides to kill herself,
he comes late into their apartment, takes off his belt
and hits her again and again, harder and harder.
Her tongueless cry is never heard.
He obliges her to have oral sex, anal sex,
whatever sex while he continues to hit her.
He is married and has three children.
She only has him, not his name.
That night she falls asleep sucking the thumb
of her left hand.

Nothing else happens. She drinks
twenty-two pills, one to ease the pain
of each year she has lived.
Like her mother when Iris was three years old.
Iris does not want to die and she doesn't.
She lives in this story as a woman who has no story.

EXCESSES
to Mami Tete

She thinks she sees me, but I know she can't.
She sees only shadows, thinks shadows
are what's real. I think I'll be blind
when I grow older. I tell her how beautiful
she is in her dress she can't see is dirty,
and those wide open green eyes I used to
be so afraid of, like the look of cats I can't read.
I still feel I can't look her in the eyes.
This fear doesn't fit my grown body. I have
too many years now, too many phone calls,
checks to write and letters to answer. Excess
of choices and complaints and pounds,
excess of power, political, of the men
that stand for years in front of countries
supposing good doses of paid favors,
corruption, "friendliness," traffic of influence
and nepotism. Excess of pleasure, consumption of drugs,
narcotraffic, excess of money for the friends
of those men sustaining a frivolous life
of expenses that shoot like barometers of survival,
in a new earth more interested in the latest edition
of status cars they can't pay for,
but borrow to pay. We finish the twentieth century
with public freedom, more beautiful, more healthy,
tonified, cosmopolitan and more comfortable,
but more and more we are slaves to our private ambitions.
Mami Tete, she has an excess of years now,
an excess of stories to tell. She is so beautiful
in her lies. I know she got married pregnant.

Once I tried to make her tell me but she was smarter
and didn't remember. Her second marriage
was with a Portuguese. He was tender.
Today he yells at her, gets furious when she's careless
and forgetful. She doesn't care.
Nothing is important for her anymore.
She doesn't look scared. Inside her I see
nothing, just those green eyes that are lit.
Her green eyes that are open even when she's
asleep. When she saw my daughter she was sorry,
"Why didn't she inherit my green eyes?" Mami Tete
asked. I wonder why she needs to feel
she is leaving. It's three-thirty
in the not-morning-yet. The smallest baby has
woken up three times. I went to take my son
to the bathroom but he was wet. I let him sleep.
At five my husband will wake up to do his exercises.
My day will start without sleep,
that small time I need to forget who I am.

A VOICE IS CRYING

A memory, the vision of a cry.
La Plaza de Mayo. Las Madres.
My son is still a baby.
I am walking on the long *calle Florida.*
An attendant in a store looks at me
and asks if I love my son.
"Of course, what do you mean?"
I saw the skin embroidery under her eyes,
the tension on her cheeks, the taints of shadows
on her forehead. Softly, not wanting to awake
her memories, I asked her again.
"I loved my son, he was so young
when they took him, only sixteen.
Come to La Plaza de Mayo this Sunday.
Bring your son." My son could not fit into my body.
He was out, bringing childless women
thoughts of their children.
I wanted to hide him, as if it was a shame
to have him alive. This woman's anger did not know
where to go. I felt afraid.

My husband did not let me go to *La Plaza de Mayo*
on that Sunday, not with our son he said.
I know they carry the photographs
of their sons hanging from their necks.
They are not dead. They are *Desaparecidos.*
Could someone recognize them and show them the way back?
Where are these *Desaparecidos?*
Are they in the same place

where the *Desaparecidos* of Pinochet are?
Where is this voice coming from?
Could it be the voice of a Jesuit in El Salvador?
Or maybe, a Sandinista dying in Nicaragua. Or a poet
writing verses with blood in a prison in Cuba.
Is it the voice of a girl slipping out of her diary,
"Dear kitty, yours Anne"?

Nationalism is the pride of having a nation.
This voice has fallen out of a mouth.
I hear it. I don't want to hear it:
Merda! Merda! Merda!

IN SEARCH OF AN ECHO

I don't know why I open
to a page
that has no lines.
I don't resist this whiteness,
this peace,
or the rounds
of guilt
hanging from an apple tree,
or the arrow
searching for center
in my head.
I want to throw a rock
into the mirror.
Maybe it will find an echo
or be devoured.

BURIED IN HER WEDDING DRESS

Only eighteen. She was buried in her wedding dress.
A wedding that never happened. A body that never made love.
A brown shadow covered her eyes, her eyes
coming out of their place, the cancer eating her.
She was defecating balls of blood. She asked the nurse
to leave her with her dirt, with the odor of old blood,
that every movement was hurting her,
that she *knew* death.
Her mother touched the floor with her lips
                                    and her tears,
asking the doctor to save her daughter. The doctor,
in the nurses' lounge, asked for coffee and wept.
The girl, only thirsty.
I have a friend who scraped off all of her hair and bought a wig
to be as her friend who has cancer. They both walk around
with new wigs and scarves adorning their necks.
But I have nothing on my head,
only this story the last nurse who bathed her told me
before I went to the maternity ward to see my sister.

She is breast-feeding her daughter.

I wonder if someone has to die to leave a space for another
to be born. If I had something on my head, a hat maybe, it is gone.

THE WINGS

Silence stands in the place of my imagination.
Things move when I see them moving. People exist
when I touch them. Memories are when I remember them.

A child is pushing the swing fast, flying.
I am that child.
The skirt of my dress is the outline of a broken umbrella,
awakening my sensations, refreshing my wet thighs
like the summer of my childhood.
Now I pull my skirt up, there I am penetrable.
I am soft on the light skin of my breasts. But
inside, deeper, where I can not see,
I can not feel.

There are silences inside me,
   the rain wetting the ocean, their indifferent dialogue,
      or the air when the swing arcs down.

ABSENCE

to Victor, in memory of our love

Drawing sketches of your eyes I imagined them
inside the holes of the eyes of the fish
bones I saw in the soup I was making last
afternoon. The holes were so perfectly round
and empty I imagined your eyes filling them —
your eyes so abruptly awakening inside
the holes of the bones of your eyes. Your face
so full of bones. Once we were on the most western
side of this island, it was there
you wanted to eat fish and I was pregnant.
And pregnant women's desires are highly respected
in this country. So I said I wanted
fish to the people that had already
said they didn't have any. They pointed to
the fishermen's boats arriving on the beach.
They had fresh countless fish in a sea full of dead
Dominicans, who run out of their country,
barefoot, on the same colorful little
boats, to die, drowning in these waters.
We bought half a dozen and they were pink.
We ate them all. I took a picture with one
of your eyes looking through the hole of a
fish's eye-bone. Oh! Your eyes, always wide
open, wider, your eyes that see too much
even in the places there's not much to see,
your eyes that hear, even through the stories
that seem superfluous, your eyes that have

materialized me, making me a woman.
I am writing sketches of your skin, the color
of the wood we built our house with. You are
so much part of the nature I admire,
always searching, moving,
restless, around the square section of
your earth. We sleep with each other, we talk
on the phone at mid-morning and at mid-day —
snack times for conversation, but I miss you.
Eating dinner tonight, our son to my left,
our sleeping daughter to my right and you,
all the way across the long round table
I could hardly hear you. I said I am
going to marry again. You round your eyes,
scared, I guess, threatening our
so-called stability. And I said yes,
marry you to have another time for us
alone. Work, children, meetings, tear me apart.
We sleep together but I miss you.

THE CHOSEN SON

Africa, 1992, a woman has to decide which
of her twin sons will die. She doesn't have enough milk
in her breasts to feed both of them, not enough to feed one.
She watches how, slowly, the chosen son
leaves his corpse of hunger.

*

Haiti, 1992, a picture of Saint Helene Saint Jean and her
six-year-old son is standing in front of me. I see the outline
of a mouth separated from a face. This hunger
is refusing translation. Wilme's teeth are claws trying to scrape
her mother's breast-burning juice. Her son's living body
is the proof of her own body. "Sometimes you just cry,
because all you can give is sympathy," said the head nurse
who gave Wilme medicine and to his mother a lecture and some bags
of cracked grain to boil for him and the other six children
she had left at home. Wilme's skin is glued to his bones.
I don't want to see this, I just want to put down
my other leg and walk away.

*

Dazilia Jean holds her one-year-old daughter Guertha,
about to be hospitalized. Dazilia is a damaged woman.
Does hunger have a sound? I ask Dazilia. "Yes, it grunts,"
she says, with an out-of-place smile, that glows in her face
with the fear of seeing her daughter resting easy

as a living baby while a cherubim sings. This is her end.
This woman has so much pride, or is it few tears left?
The wrong people are being punished.

*

San Juan, 1992, my seven-month daughter starts crying
in the middle of the night. She's hungry,
already accustomed to life, a great habit we put on,
with a growing compulsion of hunger. She cries for some seconds,
before I stand up to prepare her formula milk.
My breasts swell, I have both milks. My husband says,
"What an immense pain for a father listening to his child
cry of hunger and not having anything to give him."
I wonder which of my two children I would choose for death.
I think about Wilme and Guertha and Philippe
and Danielle Celestine, the ones I have in pictures.
They are clinging to my neck nearer than my golden necklace,
holding in the wonder of suffering. I carry them always
and everywhere. I hear the sound of their French *patois* fused
with my own voice coughing out the terror of dying.
I hold my five-year-old son. I think about Wilme.
Pienso en la palabra democracia. I dream, because dreams
are the only country from which we can never be evicted.

THE HUMMING

I rock my daughter to sleep.
From the roundness of my mouth, I hum a melody, silently.
Distracted, I stop.
She opens her eyes, moves, uncomfortable
and wants to wake me for the sound again. She looks at me
like no one has ever looked at me before.
It's night. Our eyes have grown used to the light
of this darkness. Inside me, the silence of the humming.
I am not empty, I have just been opened.

The cracked rocking sound is ringing like an alarm clock.
I wake up to the rocking of another body,
back to my third year of life.

She is caressing my chest. Her warm hand
goes through my shirt, feeling for my heart.
I am making her believe I can't breathe. She wants
to make the air flow into me. I need her.
We are alone. With her mouth closed, she makes the music
that calms me and makes me sleep.

I adored her body, warm or cold, I can't remember.
I adored her flat cheek pressed to mine in desperation.

My daughter wants to swallow me, to take me into her sleep.
But I'm too big. I've been eating the silence of this house.

And I wonder how I learned to form
with my mouth closed, this round music.

PLAYMATES IN THE BATHTUB

On Fridays the maid comes to clean this house
in the woods. These floors have no shine, made out of wood,
they get dirty easily. I'm so careless.
The kitchen has an old white sink
with twin faucets: one for the woman in the house,
the other for the same woman in the house.
The bathroom has an old toilet that flushes by pulling
a chain, a *bidet*, and right in the middle of it,
an enormous tub with golden legs.
The tub has a round plaque that reads "Birthday Bath."
I used to lay back and splash roughly
till the water jumped out of the half-full tub.
My legs pulling up my pelvic bones, pressing my uterus.
I laugh to myself feeling the baby swimming inside,
knowing I could not have her come out of me, never.
Knowing she would never break my perineum and pass
through the narrow me. I laugh feeling a certain relief.
I go up again, making my legs push strongly my body high,
feeling the strain in the veins in my thighs.

*

The maid complains I leave my bras everywhere.
I hang them on a hook the carpenter made for the bathroom.
She thinks underwear is supposed to be hidden.
But everybody can see them, they are sold in ordinary stores.
The truth is I only hide my panties, not my panties,
but the smell of my panties. I choose them pretty,
with French laces, all colors except white.
White is the color of my mother's. I hate bras.
They press too hard. I take them off all the time,

any place around the house. I hang them wide open
and she comes, complaining with her lowered voice,
folds them, hangs them again and puts a hat on top of them,
"You should not leave them like that, people can come in
and might see them, especially men" This is just a piece
of cloth, what is the matter with a man's head?
I can't believe she believes what she says. I try
not to be too hard on her and just smile. I'll keep on
hanging them wherever I please. She knows that.
She knows I'll do whatever I want in this house.
I've been pregnant too long now. I can get pregnant
in this house if I wish. But I can't give birth.
I can't give birth anymore. It hurts. Both hurts:
giving birth and not being able to give birth.

*

I have to give myself completely to this man
in a white gown. I have to put on a paper-dress opened
in the back. I can't even wear a bra.
Everyone will want to see me. They want to shave
my pubic hair. I tell them no.
Don't touch my parts. I can't even feel them,
I'm all asleep. I've been dispersed.
I just feel half of my chest and arms.
I look to the left and there's another man looking at me
as if I and my body were a curiosity. I've never seen him
but I hold both of his hands and press them. I am afraid.
I don't trust the equipment. I wonder, what if the electric
power goes out? What if there's an earthquake right now?
I try to see the opening in my womb through the crystals
of the doctor's eyeglasses. They have little drops of blood.

I want to explode. Maybe I am exploding.
My heart begins to feel pressure. I have no God
to protect me. I have been dismembered.
At the moment of my daughter's birth
I am rehearsing the moment of death.

*

I don't feel her body. She is out now.
A man is cleaning her body. A man is penetrating
her mouth, pulling her tongue out, opening her openings.
I can't explain her hands, the force of her muscles
stretching. I can't explain how she's breathing,
rhythmically, out of my body. I surrender
to her and to her beauty. She is taken away from me.
A schedule is set to see her, to feed her.

*

She will be one year soon. We call her the "Savage Girl."
She knows me already. I know who she is.
We both know our desire, to be fighting against each other,
like I am with my mother and my mother with her mother:
women against women of their own blood. I treat her
with respect. It's been weeks now that she's walking.
She looks at me from the corners of her eyes.
We have a secret. She ignores me often.
And I close my eyes. I try to make love to my body.
I become pregnant again, and I am again
in my white "Birthday Bath" pulling my pelvis up,
feeling the touch of clean water caressing my body,
feeling fresh. I take my time in the tub.
I hear no one crying yet.

MORNING MIRROR

Let me begin by saying how dependent I am
on your voice while making love.
Often I feel I am dying, I touch my body
and again I touch it.
My outer skin is of pink marble
on the bathroom floor.
Its coolness wakes me to the mirror.
I see the face of a woman aging.
I see my eyes and inside my eyes
me again. Everything seems to be me
in this morning mirror.
I open my mouth, see my teeth.
How hard I can be.

My skin feels soft
but I am dying of not feeling.
Every morning I am late to wake up.
I am entering a tunnel
without a rope around my waist.
I can fall deeply in my own mind
incarcerating those outside of me.
Killing myself makes me afraid.
In what ways would I not do it? Why crown
my body with a head if I have lost it?
I don't care about what shoes or jewelry to wear.
I want my dolls to surround me, my books
to stay open in my bedroom

my walls to be pink when they are blue.
I want to stay in this room with this mirror
to feel the veins of the marble tiles,
to feel your veins, worms through my body.
I want to urinate and listen to its sound.
To bite you and feel it in my tongue.

NO BUTTER FOR BREAKFAST

for the Cuba of September, 1993,
and the friends I met.

I had to open my eyes.
It had to be there, where each face is a caravel
with sinking eyes, broken.
There, floating over the sea,
a blue mantle where they bury themselves,
I urinated on the urine of others —
as if a family, a great human family.

What do I know, why am I here, at this moment in history?

No toilet paper. Butter for breakfast
is nonexistent but it's not necessary because
the bread for breakfast doesn't exist.
Taking pictures, I overheard a woman, *what a pity, Señora,*
that hunger can not come out in pictures.
I wasn't hungry then, only floating.

ON BEING LOST

My head is bent, but my eyes are looking up.
I am going to be crazy. Soon language will be
my own invention transcending the alphabet,
the birds' songs, the noises from nature.
I am writing poetry, bending my head
with my eyes looking up
to nowhere or to somewhere
where I can locate a memory
that brings me back into something old, or common.
I don't wash my hair. Its oil is spilling
on my forehead, making it shine. It's not dirt.
It comes from me.
I am in a state of lethargy,
reaching into nothing, lost.
I know I can be mad if I want to,
it's easy. But I never choose the easy path.
I hear noises that resemble children's voices.
Maybe these children are making noises to awaken me.
But I want to sleep. I need to sleep.
It's more complicated than being mad,
than not letting anyone enter into my understanding.
That's easy.
I can do that without being crazy.
I can be sane and not let anyone enter my reality,

that is never anyone else's reality.
The noise is louder. It fills my *axilas* and opens my holes.
I think those are children.
From where do they come? From whom do they come?
Are they inside my womb or my head?
This morning I wake up
feeling agitated without having touched my body.
I'm smiling. Children are making noises,
but I need to be left alone, whoever I am.

REPOSING

Only the waters of the lagoon move.
I see through the sliding door
little waves these waters curl into,
how the wind, the softest wind of the night
tenders this liquid mass that connects me
with the unknown. Waters connecting us all,
our continents, our countries,
our small niches, corners we call houses.
There's only silence
at this enormous hour of the night.
I must be awaiting something.
But I don't need anything,
the waters will always be there,
uncapturable. She can drink us,
we can disappear in one of her angers.
And then, again, she is there,
exhaling, a wide bed
waiting for someone to sleep with her.
Waters, to die into.

LIKE A ROCK

The baby is sleeping.
It's not dawn yet.
I am waiting for the beginning of a New Day.
Why this restless need to look at myself in the mirror
　and feel different?

I will cross the valley and bounce into the cold lake
　to sense my sleeping flesh.
I haven't been touched for so long, I hardly remember.

Faced in front of this huge body of water,
I take off my clothes, slowly, diligently,
　as one does when wanting to intensify the moment of love.

First I unbutton my skirt.
It slips carelessly down to the sodden grass.
My underwear is humid.
I move close to the water. I start to see the first liquid
　fingers shelter my cold feet.
With a silenced soul, I came here to feel.
I am holding this moment.
Without resistance, I give up.

The water is arctic but not indifferent, coming in full-
　motion waves to dance with my nudity.
The water is fingering my intangible body.

My breasts awaken. I become scared.
I feel the touch inside my body and
  I don't know if my soul exists.
Tears come down my cheeks.
I am not sure where these come from:
  if it is dew, or the lake, or a delirium.
I can not discern the difference:
  if my soul cries, if my eyes cry,
    or both, or none.

I rise out of the water. My hair floats.
I face the wind, feeling like a miniature Victory of Samothrace.
I tighten my arms and become frigid: unmoved, a rock,
  with this obstinacy of mine of not belonging to this race,
  of not needing nor wanting to be held.

The baby is crying.

RACHEL

Two men are holding me in my room —
one is my doctor who kissed me when I was still pretty
and young and wanted to be kissed.
He's dressed as a policeman.
The other is pulling my panties down.
He's a businessman and wants to have something with me.
He has a knife in his right hand. I can't move.

I hear voices calling me:
"Drug addict, prostitute, alcoholic.
Take off your clothes and go to the streets."
Running, I go to my neighbor's house to answer the voices,
my voices, the voices I hear that say the wishes I want.

On the brown sofa of my female psychiatrist,
I am not afraid. My arms are being tied.
I see a man, white, with a syringe in his hands.
Through it I see a thick crystal liquid.
I'm scared, but the fear is not beyond me.
Fears of others who are themselves afraid.

I am awake and still I am dreaming —
I can see them, they are the two men crucified with Christ.
One holding me at my right, the other at my left.
Good and bad, to the right and to the left.
Which is whom? And so I wonder

which direction do the horses run?

AMBIVALENT PREGNANCY

August. My daughter was born in August.
She was not so much desired as decided.
It was devastating being pregnant
throughout that whole angry summer —
hot, humid, heavy.
And then the delivery: the catheter, the waiting
in that room with paper dressing our bodies.
Three women waiting for Caesareans,
laughing scars forever below our bellies.

Not so much desired as decided,
she was born after paying two hundred and fifty dollars
for an abortion. The doctor in the clinic came in
too late for me. I had been waiting all morning
with women sitting in a circle, needing to tell
their different stories. Listening to them confess,
forgiving themselves,
convinced me I didn't have a story.

I wonder about all those babies who will never smile
or be six months old like my daughter tomorrow.
Those babies will not get hurt or abused
or tied to the pillar of a bed
and obliged to practice fellatio on the Catholic priest
of her town, when she turned fifteen
and was more beautiful than her sisters.

I wonder if she really wanted to be born
from an unhappy mother, striving so much to find herself
but finding someone else moving inside her.
And what if one day she imagines me taking her
out of my body but desires it
as I thought my mother should have done with me?

I cried and cried and cried
to be clean for that fifth day of August.
I am born, I think, through her.
It wasn't that she was desired
but I decided her at the precise moment
when they called my name.

BLACK SUN

I am left alone
to clean the dishes,
to fix the bed
and take the dirt out of this place.

Left on this rainy morning of September,
to think out loud of my whereabouts
and drink some coffee with my soul.

I am alone with this black sun
in a solo piece of music with the rain.
Entirely for myself, to play with my old dolls.
I empty my face of all human reminders
to learn to be a part of the larger farce.

SOUNDS

I close the door
to be alone. I don't like to close doors.
I close the door to be alone inside this blue
chamber of tapestries
of Victorian white nightgowns
hanging from the old mahogany clothier.
Watching the empty bed of fragrances
of human flesh
I hear the waters in noises
lullabying the dead wooden boats
already greenish from lichens and moss.
My son far, my daughter far.
The sounds of their voices are the air
slipping from under the door.
The man gone a long time ago
to recapture the other one
opening in his pale eyelids.
The man closing his eyes beneath
the thought of himself
dead for ever.
Out of the water, out of the nowhere
the noises move
foaming my windows,
hitting my glass.
The noises want
to enter into my voice.
Or is it the voice
entering into the noise?

THE COLOR OF MY EYES

When my son and I were waiting
for the elevator and the door opened
I saw nothing inside.
My son was rushing to get in
and I let him go, fearing he would fall
into an abyss.
And when in my mind he was ready to fall,
at that instant
when his right leg was suspended in the air,
I looked again and saw that I was wrong,
that I had misunderstood my senses.
He did not fall.
He went down to his father
who was taking him to the first floor
of his life, kindergarten.

Or it is this fantasy of mine of going up
on top of the highest building, to play
with the wind in its open space,
to make believe I want to throw myself off.
I wait with my right leg suspended in the air
till my father appears. My arms
are holding my body from the fence.
I am getting ready to let go.
I just want to see my father's eyes,
then I'll stop the game.

Feeling this is strenuous for me.
Like this pink color covering everything
in the room. It is not my bedroom
that I imagine. I have never lived in this place,
but I can not rip it out. All pink.
I only have to close my eyes and it appears,
well lighted. A light on near the bed,
right above it. A light on the beige desk
full of papers and open books, abandoned,
half-glanced at. The bed with a pink and lilac
bedspread, two huge pillows matching the fabric.
Pink the rugs, pink the walls,
no longer a color but the pink of obsession.
I am not who I think I was,
no longer in control of the movements
of my hands and the rhythm of my words.
I do not know anymore the language that I speak
or in what language I dream.

I am not the woman with hard breasts
and wide, strong, fertile hips.
My eyes are not the eyes of the girl I was,
green like an olive after being submerged in vinegar,
a sour crying color. Dark green like wet grass.
I can no longer believe my eyes
nor what my heart feels,
wherever the thoughts are hidden.

For many years I had a ring on.
It was only after taking it off that I saw
its mark in my skin and knew it was enough.
I no longer believed in gold or silver.
It is this elevator opening and closing,
the pink room covered with paper-flowers,
this ring I want off my finger
which will not come off.
I see my son's fear
when there is nothing to be scared of,
the room so empty this terrible color
wants to wash over it.

THE KINGDOM OF PRETENSES

Women have taken out their French porcelain dinnerwares,
silverwares, glasswares and have decorated their dining
table for their men. And there, white linen Swedish napkins
for mouth's delightfulness. Oh, and here they come
in their coquettish attires,
swinging around their worked hips for everyone's contemplation.
You've always eulogized such type of women.

A delusion of womanhood, and feminism, and macholess attitude:
here I stand. Me, the simple careless me that I could be,
without curling my hair, with my face blank, with
colorless eyelids. Forgotten my wedding rings,
my diamond earrings, my birthday present pendant.

No culinary ambitions, nor precisely
interested in jewelry, nor listening to you
applaud another woman. I am perplexed, useless
to these things not appealing to me. Not even in your tired sex,
late at night, when you come from work, to sleep
with your young wife you think you have treated like a queen.

Blessings for the lovers like you! They never lose their head.
They take them with them to be fully, gloatingly conscious
of their own and of their partners' alienation.

There are times when you burlesque me about all I do not know,
the identity of an author, the title of a novel,
the name of the secretary of state, or in any case,
your secretary's name.

I have more of the common things an ordinary woman
will be appeased with, but I am not happy.
Only let me hang some few paintings on the entrance wall,
let me occupy a space with my old books, let me leave
my corpse once in a while in your presence.
And if my silences make you go,
I will be here drawing words and painting phrases.
I will be here destroyed, inhuman, but here . . .
afraid of closing my eyes I might forget how to open them
and never ever see this round body of mine
or recognize my face in the mirror.

It's not that you're losing me.
I am losing myself.

BECOMING A WOOD

The sky is ash, that color of the moon passing through the clouds.
I can die on a day like this. The breeze at the closing door of
  this house,
brings me inside the unsound wind I felt the day he made us
  leave him, mother, sister and I.

That wind trimmed part of my body, framing my future,
following me in my own substitutions,
one deception, then another.

Now I am here in this house of naked wood, and I am this house,
  and I am this wood,
chambered by the roof of this foliage.

BRUTE MYSTERY

for Victorino Paolo

My son is learning to draw triangles,
rectangles, circles.
He is learning to recognize his fingers
by their names.
He is learning to draw numbers
while he discovers the jumpiness in his hand
when prolonging the lines on the white sheet.
Such wrinkled little fingers, my son has.
His fingernails always filled with dirt.
Only three and already questioning life:
one, two, three; Papa, Mama, boy;
"*Where do I come from? Where is Papa?*
Why do we always have to be alone?
Will you always be with me, Mama? Why
do I get scared at night? Why do I wet my bed?"
What can I answer? I have my own questions.
I gaze distracted, openmouthed, out of the window
by the gallery. From the fifth floor where we live,
people seem so tiny and archaic, dwarfed by the great
violet sky. We move to a windy corner and a spray
blows on our faces carrying the smell of coffee
from the south of the island.
This tropical air has seeped into the earth
transforming me — earthbound — a worm trapped
in a blue cave. There, the open sea,
the unknown, my excuse for becoming distracted

from his queries. He knows this.
We give each other a kiss or rather we press
our cheeks, entertained by the clouds
framing monster with the air. Then, that sky,
a hundred and eighty degrees of brute mystery.

THE PILE OF SAND

An accident. My son could be dead.
My husband could be dead and you come to say it was
an accident? Can someone tell me the meaning of this word?
Can you believe the sound of a gigantic ball of steel
in your backyard on a Sunday when you think nothing happens.
We were eating words and making stories in the dining room
of our house in the country. Husband and son had just come up
into the house when that tremendously shocking noise
of big crash — a car — had just jumped in over the fence
way down into my backyard. The man lost control of his car:
said the door went open and when he was closing it
the car threw him out. An accident?
I didn't even want to look at the car, color of shit,
stuck in that pile of dirt I had hated for months
on a nice sunny boring Sunday. Husband, as usual, has made
unconcerned attention to evict each grain of dirt, the dirt
is really sand which in my terms means the same. He claims
it could be of use to make slabs of concrete he keeps putting
everywhere on the farm. It has baby-sat my son and his dwarf
friends who dig canals and bury each kind of Tonka truck,
plastic cow, horse, pig, spacing the sand to the extensions
of my forehead. The big boy keeps judiciously putting back
the sand in a big pile. Son keeps spacing the sand. Father
keeps putting it back together in a well-shaped small mountain.
I keep looking through the window like a far spectator.
Didn't say much. Didn't verbally protest.
One doing, the other undoing. One big, the other small.
One spacing the sand, the other putting it back together,
playing. When I heard the crane bringing the car out of the yard,
I took a curious look. There it was, unmovable,
permanent, that pile of sand in the backyard.

THE LIGHT OF THE MOON

The little girl crawls to the glass.
She sees an image and laughs and says *titi*.
That primitive language communicates her wholly.
She looks at the portrait of the baby
hanging on the wall across from the mirror
and laughs and says *titi*.
She doesn't know that both are her,
that she is someone.
What is reflected in the mirror
is enough for her to laugh and play,
but she knows that the one in the mirror
is the same as the one in the portrait.
She feels I am important to her.
Whenever a stranger comes she hugs my legs,
hiding, until she gets used to the image
of a new human or animal. It doesn't matter to her,
human or animal. Everything that moves is the same.
The other night, I showed her *la luna*,
unmoving, round, among all the little lights.
She learned what *la luna* is.
She goes outside, when it's night,
and with her finger pointing up
she looks at me and smiles and stays still.
On her face the light of *la luna*.
Now when I want to calm her, even in daytime,
I say *la luna* and she looks at me. I tell her,
yes, it's there, but the very light of the sun
keeps it from us, but yes, it's there,
look, somewhere in the sky.

A TASTE OF IRONY

Since this morning I have had a feeling you could taste,
a bitterness on the sides of your mouth.
I woke up from a dream I can't remember.

I have had my hair cut short and a perm to curl it.
I had a striped short dress with no bra on. I hated bras.
I still do. That sensation of feeling the clothes
pressed to my fourteen-year-old nude breasts felt good
and satisfying. Standing in the kitchen, preparing lunch,
he came in and saw me with my new look.
You are so ugly I doubt very much you will ever marry.
I don't think anyone will fall in love with you.
Suffering alone, I felt stripped by invisible hands,
defense after defense, garment after garment,
until I was stark naked.
I had to put my lunch inside the refrigerator.

This scene was lived again a month after I met the man
who was to be my husband. I was still in that trance
of hypnotic stare, in love, where things turn blurry.
He came into the house, *that man, such an important person,*
what would he want from you, you have nothing to offer him,
not a woman enough to be with a man like that.

But I knew the taste of that instant.

THE SUN ITSELF

This flat exhaustion of daily going down
only to come up again. For what purpose did I come here?
To look at the deep colors of green changing the profile
of the mountains while the sun's distorting light
becomes shadow on them? I'm bored even with myself
and my uncaged mind. What I want is something I have yet
not known. Something I want someone to show me,
to be surprised with,

and the day, perhaps, could be safe.

I want to feel the space that is more than a mockery,
an angle to look at without being hurt. Today I woke
out of my sleep and my burning head. I drove
an hour to leave the routine of *things I must do* in the day.
To be the daughter of the sun, a jealous daughter
who watches her father's shadow
to pretend I'm not watching him . . . Gone.
In the dream he was wearing a ponytail, in last night's
dream he wasn't there. I don't want him to be there.
But my mother reminds me that he will always be her only love.

Why is this still important to me? Why be
the daughter of the sun and not the sun itself?

Maybe I came here because I needed to stop the talk.
My head burns. I don't know how to control my blood,

to rest, to sleep and not to die,
to close my eyes, touch my eyelids, move the balls of the eyes,
massage the eyelids with the tips of my fingers.

And now it's just raining for the mountains,
in this late returning.

THE SILENCE BEFORE

I am thinking about the few moments one really has
of silence. Not the silence one makes when a plane is departing,
nor the silence lovers make when their eyes meet,
but last night's silence of exhaustion after love.

I am thinking about that woman waiting in the hospital.
Not the one I went to see, whose body had the smell
of bodies close to death. But about that other woman.
Her eyes, moons in grief.
She glanced to nowhere. I am thinking about her skin,
how it changed, how sadness is not black
but yellow. And I saw her womanhood parallel to mine,
her fragility strong against my health and youth.
Then, that last silence

standing there paralyzing the passage of my thoughts,
the lines on my skin from deepening. That silence
inside her scented cave.

I did nothing, thought nothing.
I want to tell God he's guilty, but I don't think about God.
I want to say I am innocent, but no one is accusing me.
I waited for the elevator. When it opened,
her eyes, the way she moved them to avoid mine
were already memory.

THE SWIMMER

I come out of the water and start jogging.
My body athletic. I'm tall and muscular.
I jog, stronger at each step, flying.
I move heavy and secure
                touching barefoot the humid tileless floor.

In my dreams I always see myself with dark hair.

My dress is of two pieces, a high-cut thigh bikini,
and a bra very tight to my breasts
so they do not fall. I'm sweating.
I don't know how long I've been jogging.
Here I am standing
at the edge of the trampoline.
The water is turbid.
I'm throwing myself. A perfect throw.
My body perfect.
The water is refreshing.
I hear the sound of a voice speaking my name,
inside the swimming pool, through the water.
The voice is clear,
                but not human.

I am breathing water.
                I am drinking the air.

LEGENDS OF THE MIND

Suddenly, listening to someone call my name
starts to sound strange. This name
given to me, out of where?
And then, after this name, a borrowed one.
It's no wonder why women are so lost.
This man, calling me this morning,
accenting my name on the last vowel.
My brother, instead, stressing more the first.
What is the sound of my name? How should I say it?
Is it my mom's backwards really?
Did my father hate her so much, he invented
her upside-down, out from a wound,
the third knife cut. And there I was,
an invention, a mistake of sounds.
I'm so fed up with this name, so bored
of this hair and this skin. What if
I were born black and with violet eyes,
would I have the same name and the same
damn heart? Would I have this same grand forehead
and my thick eyebrows? I'm so fed up
with the suffering of this world,
the glory of pain. I too want to die —   ·
but I'm stuck here in this blue cage
with these white linen sheets and golden liquids
from Champagne. I'm forced to look
at the Reims Cathedral, immaculate.
Compelled to see the broken columns of the Parthenon,
and hate Mikonos with its white breast-like shades.
I'm tired, tired, tired.

I don't want to hear another cry
or visit an agonizing tomb.
What about kings and queens or the beauty
of the coast of Monaco? What about learning
from the Indians, who died carrying the rocks up, high,
constructing a Machu-Pichu of extra-terrestrial inventiveness?
What about the men who are not from this earth?
Plato, Christ, Mohammed, who else rose?
I'm bored, bored, fed up with the legends of the mind.
Do I have to love this name and stick with it till I die?
Does it have ears or a mouth?

IN A TRANCE

The pencil moves at a thought
acknowledging only the poorness of the human soul.
Yes, I have to speak of soul and I have to include my *I*
because it is me who moves the pencil
me who thinks the thoughts
                        and closes her eyes
to listen to the rain on the zinc ceiling
swinging herself in a *hamaca*
caring for nothing
imagining how happy the flowers must be
how light the wood must feel.

I remember once I was feeling light
as if I were part of the air, alive but leaving.

Isn't it the truth, I mean that ultimate truth, realizing one's
   existence?

That woman makes herself dizzy
and she pushes the table with her feet to swing even faster.
Nothing else is there but her body, her thoughts,
and in her thoughts her private legend, the entire universe.

HIGH FEVER

My daughter is burning with fever.
We are alone, lying on my bed.
The TV off, the air conditioner on,
the curtains half open.
The afternoon is falling,
bright oranges turning into dark orange,
blue, lilac, a soft yellow.
The big egg spreading, like magma
from the mouth of a volcano, arms wide
into the horizontal line that burns,
then it stops burning
into darkness.
My daughter sleeps.
She changes positions with my body.
Accommodates her head on my waist,
then on my chest.
I cover her with my left arm.
I put my ear on her forehead,
to feel the hot,
to listen to her dreams, her desires,
if at two she can desire something.
Her head burns.
The sun, descending from my window.
What a moment this is! The room quiet,
my eyes open to her deep breathing,
accelerating and decelerating,
dreaming alone, still
and happy.
Her fever keeps us together.

This book was set in Schneidler, printed on acid-free Mohawk Superfine paper, and bound with a Strathmore wrapper. The label was printed by Paul Mendes Letter Press of Provincetown and glued by hand to the wrapper.

Thirteen hundred and fifty copies were printed for a paper edition.

One hundred fifty copies were hardbound with a tipped-in monoprint by Michelle Weinberg.

The hardbound copies are numbered and signed by the author and the artist.